A monastery sits on the island Mont Saint-Michel off the coast of France.

Visitors to Bayon Temple in Cambodia travel by elephant.

LITTLE KIDS FIRST BIG BOOK OF THE WORLD

ELIZABETH CARNEY

NATIONAL GEOGRAPHIC KiDS

WASHINGTON, D.C.

CONTENTS

INTRODUCTION	6
HOW TO USE THIS BOOK	7
MAP OF THE WORLD	8

CHAPTER ONE
NORTH AMERICA	10
THE COUNTRIES	12
THE LAND	14
THE WEATHER	16
THE PEOPLE	18
THE ANIMALS	20
THE SIGHTS	22
LET'S GO!	
SING IN 3 LANGUAGES	24

CHAPTER TWO
SOUTH AMERICA	26
THE COUNTRIES	28
THE LAND	30
THE WEATHER	32
THE PEOPLE	34
THE ANIMALS	36
THE SIGHTS	38
LET'S GO!	
MAKE A RAIN FOREST	40

CHAPTER THREE
EUROPE	42
THE COUNTRIES	44
THE LAND	46
THE WEATHER	48
THE PEOPLE	50
THE ANIMALS	52
THE SIGHTS	54
EXPLORER SPOTLIGHT:	
CARSTEN PETER	56
LET'S GO!	
BE AN ARTIST LIKE	
MICHELANGELO	58

CHAPTER FOUR
ASIA	60
THE COUNTRIES	62
THE LAND	64
THE WEATHER	66
THE PEOPLE	68
THE ANIMALS	70
THE SIGHTS	72
LET'S GO!	
DESIGN A MOSAIC	74

CHAPTER FIVE
AFRICA	76
THE COUNTRIES	78
THE LAND	80
THE WEATHER	82
THE PEOPLE	84
THE ANIMALS	86
THE SIGHTS	88
EXPLORER SPOTLIGHT: JANE GOODALL	90
LET'S GO! WATCH ANIMALS LIKE A SCIENTIST	92

CHAPTER SIX
AUSTRALIA	94
THE COUNTRIES	96
THE LAND	98
THE WEATHER	100
THE PEOPLE	102
THE ANIMALS	104
THE SIGHTS	106
LET'S GO! LEAP LIKE A KANGAROO	108

CHAPTER SEVEN
ANTARCTICA	110
THE LAND	112
THE WEATHER	114
THE ANIMALS	116
EXPLORER SPOTLIGHT: ROALD AMUNDSEN	118
LET'S GO! TAKE CARE OF A PENGUIN "EGG"	120
PARENT TIPS	122
GLOSSARY	124
INDEX	126
CREDITS	127

The information in this book is provided for informational purposes only. Please note that some of the activities may be considered strenuous. If the reader has a medical problem or health concern, he or she should consult a medical professional before engaging in any activities.

INTRODUCTION

Would you like to learn about the whole world without leaving this very spot? You can with this atlas! An atlas is a book of maps. What is a map anyway? It's a drawing of a place as it looks from above. This book has maps of the world's continents. You'll see the shapes, locations, and features of Earth's seven major landmasses. On pages 8 and 9, you will see examples of maps that show the land and places on Earth. An atlas usually gives you more information than just maps. In this book, you'll find out about each continent's countries, land and weather, people, animals, and major sights.

NATIONAL GEOGRAPHIC'S *LITTLE KIDS FIRST BIG BOOK OF THE WORLD* IS ORGANIZED BY CONTINENT, FEATURING EVERYTHING A YOUNG EXPLORER NEEDS TO LEARN THE LAY OF THE LAND:

COUNTRIES
Discover maps that present the countries of our world and learn which nations are considered the largest and smallest of their continent.

LAND AND WEATHER
Discover a variety of landscapes with land maps that illustrate each continent's peaks and valleys, waterways and grasslands, and learn about the different types of weather and seasons around the globe.

PEOPLE
Learn about the diverse groups of people who live on each continent. Find out where they came from and how they got there.

ANIMALS
Discover some of the most interesting animals that live on each continent and find out where they make their homes, what they eat, and more.

SIGHTS
Uncover the world's most fascinating sights and the history behind their famous existence.

EXPLORER SPOTLIGHTS
Meet some amazing explorers on missions of discovery around the world and see what they have found.

HOW TO USE THIS BOOK

FACT BOXES give a quick look at important information about a continent. How many countries does it have? Which one is the smallest? Which is the biggest? Which city has the most people? You'll find the answers in the fact boxes.

POP-UP FACTS offer tidbits of really cool information. Use these to impress your friends and family with your geo knowledge.

THE COUNTRIES
An icy north and a tropical south

You'll find palm trees and sunshine on the Caribbean islands. The United States, Canada, and Mexico make up most of North America.

The land between Mexico and South America is often called Central America.

Where is the world's largest island? It's icy Greenland to the northeast of Canada.

A MALE ELK IN CANADA

Can you see how this continent is shaped like a triangle?

NORTH AMERICA

Both North and South America were named after the Italian explorer Amerigo Vespucci.

Map Key
- Country capital
- City
- Ruin
- Boundary

FACTS
COUNTRIES
23
LARGEST COUNTRY
Canada
SMALLEST COUNTRY
St. Kitts and Nevis
CITY WITH THE MOST PEOPLE
Mexico City, Mexico. About 21 million people live here.*

*Note: Population figure represents that of the metropolitan area.

QUESTIONS relate the information back to you and your life. They can even start a conversation.

LET'S GO! At the end of each section you'll find activities to try, each involving art, science, math, writing, or a physical activity.

PARENT TIPS in the back of this book provide games, activities, and project ideas. Parents can use these tips to help kids make more geography connections. There's also a glossary, a list of words and their meanings.

MAP OF THE WORLD

MAPS tell you what a place is like, even if you've never been there. Maps can also help you get where you want to go. They often use drawings called **symbols** to show things. A **map key** tells you what those symbols mean.

For example, a black solid line means the boundary between countries. A black dot stands for a city. If you don't know what a symbol on a map means, check the map key.

See larger continental maps in this book for more detail.

There are two main types of maps. **Political maps** show the outlines of countries. They can also mark the location of cities and capitals. **Physical maps** are the second type of map. These maps show an area's land and water features. You can see the locations of mountain ranges, forests, deserts, plains, and bodies of water such as lakes, rivers, and oceans.

CHAPTER 1
NORTH AMERICA

A BISON HERD IN ALBERTA, CANADA

Land of many landscapes

THE COUNTRIES

An icy north and a tropical south

You'll find palm trees and sunshine on the Caribbean islands. The United States, Canada, and Mexico make up most of North America.

The land between Mexico and South America is often called Central America.

Where is the world's largest island? It's icy Greenland to the northeast of Canada.

A MALE ELK IN CANADA

Can you see how this continent is shaped like a triangle?

THE LAND

Forests cover much of North America.

Near the North Pole, the land and ocean are often frozen. The flat land in the central plains is great for farming.

KULUSUK, GREENLAND

In the southwest, you'll find deserts and rocky canyons. Steamy jungles grow in the southern part of the continent.

ARCHES NATIONAL PARK, UTAH, U.S.A.

This type of cactus can live up to 200 years!

SAGUARO CACTUS IN ARIZONA, U.S.A.

More tornadoes form in the United States than anywhere else on Earth.

A BEACH IN TULUM, MEXICO

THE WEATHER

Hot in the south, chilly in the north

In the south, it's warm year-round, and many days are sunny!

Farther north, seasons bring cool autumn weather and rainy springs. It's cold all the time in the northernmost part of the continent. The ground is always frozen.

THE PEOPLE

People from all over the world have moved here.

GIRLS IN GUATEMALA

More than 8,000 years ago, people from Asia made their way across a land bridge to North America. More recently, people from all over the world have settled here. That's why North America has many different cultures.

People celebrate where they're from with parades, festivals, and sporting events.

Basketball was invented in North America in 1891.

A BASKETBALL GAME IN PENNSYLVANIA, U.S.A.

Kids go tobogganing (a type of sledding) in Nunavut, Canada's northernmost territory.

NORTH AMERICA

NUNAVUT, CANADA

MOTHER AND BABY POLAR BEARS

Manatees have fingernails on their front flippers.

NORTH AMERICA

THE ANIMALS
From musk oxen to manatees

Many types of animals live in North America. Some, like musk oxen and polar bears, are built for the cold. You can find manatees in waters of the warm south.

MUSK OX

SQUIRREL MONKEY

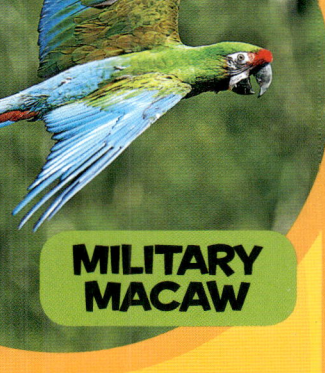
MILITARY MACAW

Parrots and monkeys squawk and screech in the rain forests of Central America.

THE SIGHTS

Old stone pyramids and a monumental gift

GRAND CANYON, U.S.A.

North America has many natural wonders, like the Grand Canyon. There are man-made ones, too.

CHICHÉN ITZÁ, MEXICO

The Maya people of Mexico and northern Central America built great stone pyramids long ago. These pyramids still stand today.

NORTH AMERICA

The Statue of Liberty stands in New York Harbor. France gave it to the United States as a gift.

The Statue of Liberty stands 305 feet (93 m) tall.

A symbol most people aren't able to see: Lady Liberty has a broken chain wrapped around her feet. It stands for the freedom that people find in the United States.

23

LET'S GO!
Sing in three languages

Most North Americans speak Spanish, English, or French. Try singing "Frère Jacques" in the three primary languages of North America.

Fray Felipe
(Spanish)

Fray Felipe, Fray Felipe,
¿Duermes tú? ¿Duermes tú?
¡Suenan las campanas!
¡Suenan las campanas!
Ding, dang, dong. Ding, dang, dong.

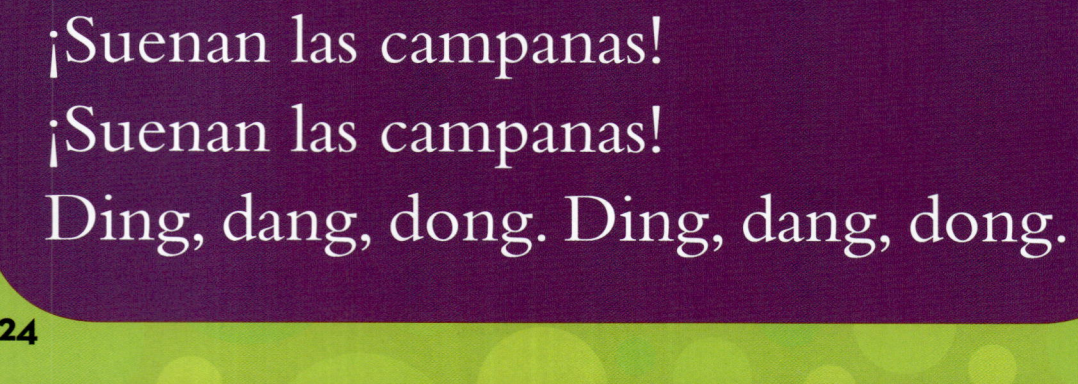

NORTH AMERICA

Frère Jacques
(French)

Frère Jacques, Frère Jacques,
Dormez-vous? Dormez-vous?
Sonnez les matines! Sonnez les matines!
Ding, dang, dong. Ding, dang, dong.

Brother John
(English)

Are you sleeping, are you sleeping,
Brother John? Brother John?
Morning bells are ringing!
Morning bells are ringing!
Ding, dang, dong.
Ding, dang, dong.

CHAPTER 2
SOUTH AMERICA

A JAGUAR IN BRAZIL

This continent is home to the world's largest rain forest and its driest desert.

THE COUNTRIES
From big Brazil to small Suriname

South America has 12 countries. Farming is important here.

Many foods come from this continent. Potatoes, tomatoes, and bananas are a few.

Most big cities are near the coasts.

A BEACH IN RIO DE JANEIRO, BRAZIL

THE LAND

The world's longest mountain range and its second longest river are here.

The Andes mountain range stretches down the west side of South America. Some of these mountains are volcanoes!

The Amazon River is very long. It snakes through the Amazon rain forest.

AMAZON RIVER

Parts of the Atacama Desert haven't seen a drop of rain since people began keeping weather records 400 years ago!

LOS FLAMENCOS NATIONAL RESERVE, CHILE

The Atacama Desert in Chile is the driest place on Earth.

The ice fields at Glaciers National Park in Argentina are the largest outside of Antarctica.

GLACIERS NATIONAL PARK, PATAGONIA, ARGENTINA

SOUTH AMERICA

THE WEATHER

Rain forest bound? Bring your umbrella!

It's hot and rainy in the northern half of South America. The Amazon rain forest is here. Parts of the forest get up to nine feet (2.7 m) of rain a year.

The southern tip of South America is very cold. That's because it's so far away from the Equator. Giant ice sheets cover some parts of the land there.

TUMUCUMAQUE NATIONAL PARK, BRAZIL

The Amazon rain forest is the largest tropical rain forest in the world.

THE PEOPLE

Olá! Hola! That's how most people say "hello" in South America.

PERUVIAN GIRL

Very long ago, people made their way from Asia across North America into South America. Over time, they built great cities. People from Europe and Africa came later.

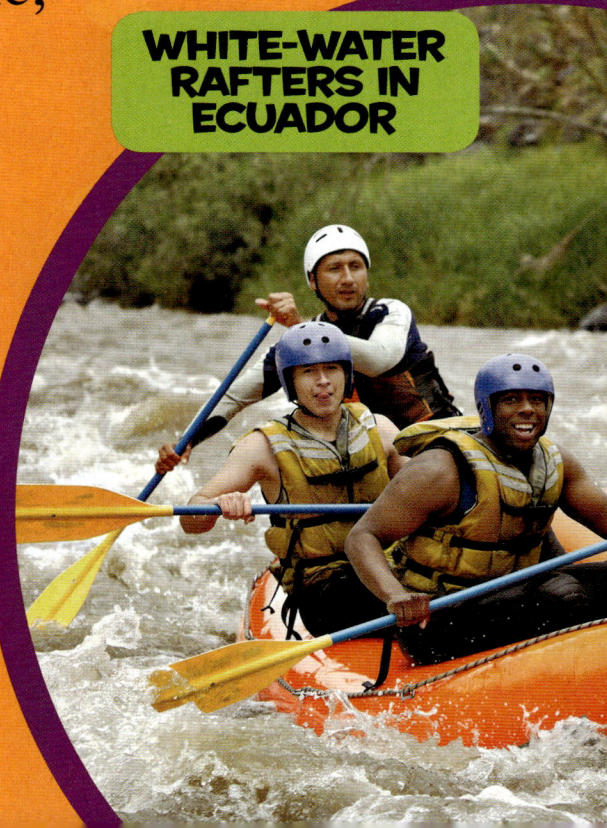
WHITE-WATER RAFTERS IN ECUADOR

Today, most South Americans are related to Asian, European, or African groups. Portuguese and Spanish are the main languages.

SOUTH AMERICA

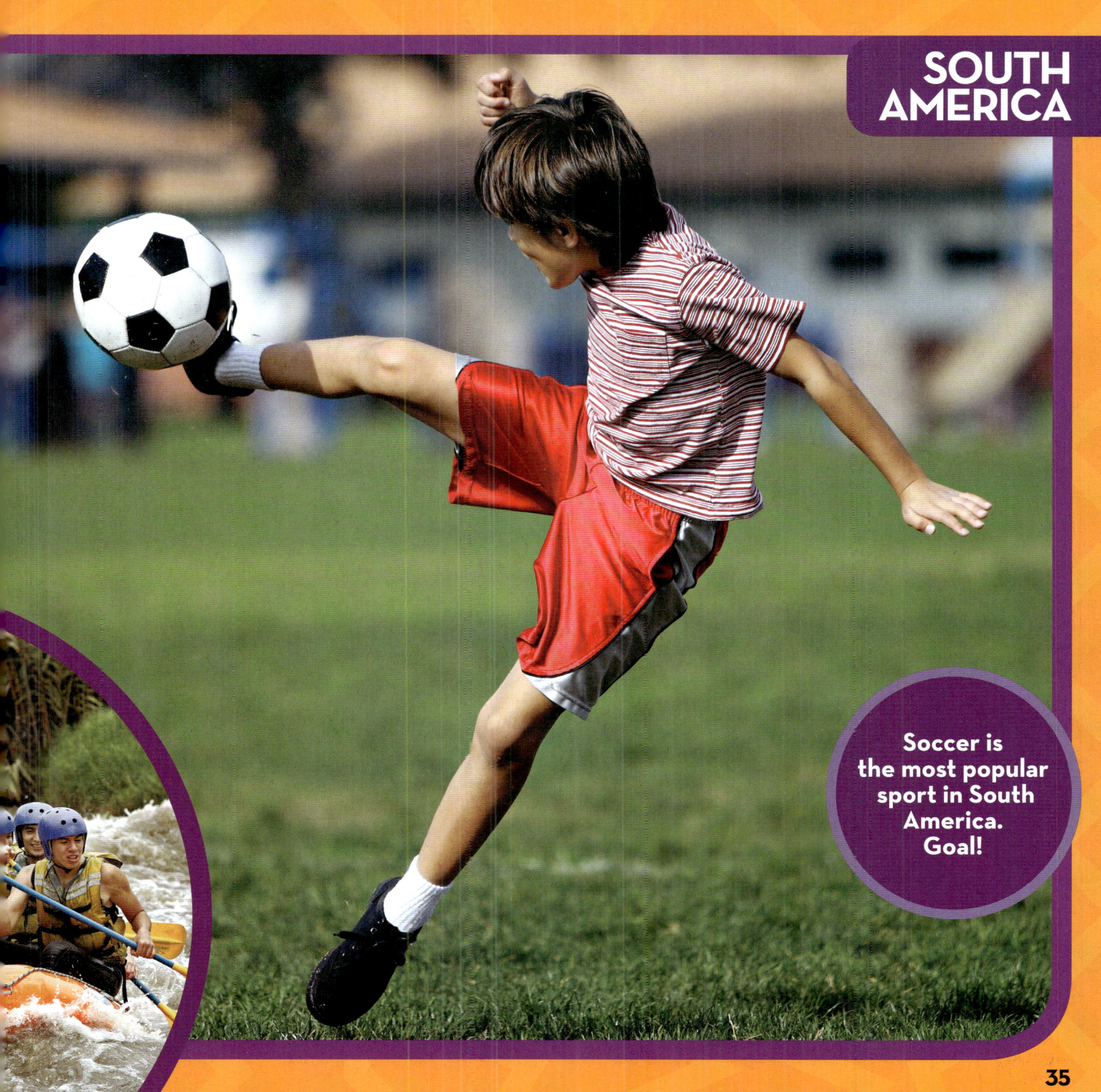

Soccer is the most popular sport in South America. Goal!

Guanacos are related to camels. They live on the plains, plateaus, and coastlines of Peru, Chile, and Argentina. They also live in the Andes.

ARMADILLO

A type of parrot, the blue-and-yellow macaw has a powerful beak for cracking nuts and seeds.

SOUTH AMERICA

THE ANIMALS
Critters in a rainbow of colors

A wide variety of animals live in South America. There are blue-and-yellow macaws, poison dart frogs, and pink river dolphins in the rain forest.

POISON DART FROG

PINK RIVER DOLPHIN

You'll find llamas in the mountains. Armadillos live in different areas of the continent.

37

THE SIGHTS
Hiking boots and dancing shoes

Travelers hike a long way to see stone ruins on a mountaintop in Peru. The site is called Machu Picchu. It's known as the Lost City of the Inca. The Inca were ancient South American people.

A CARNIVAL FESTIVAL

Many South Americans celebrate Carnival. It's a festive season, usually in February. In Rio de Janeiro, Brazil, people wear colorful costumes and dance in the streets.

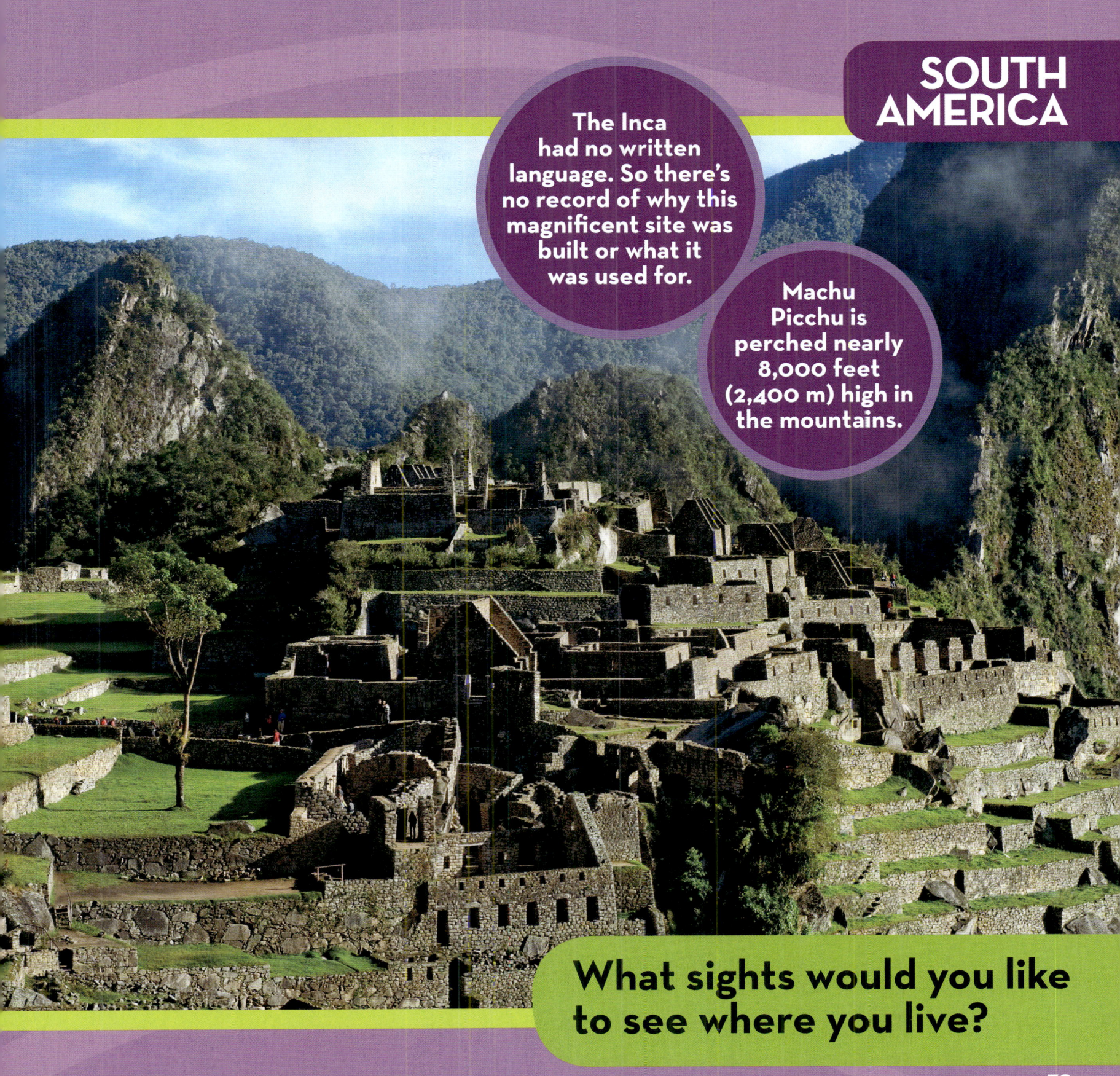

SOUTH AMERICA

The Inca had no written language. So there's no record of why this magnificent site was built or what it was used for.

Machu Picchu is perched nearly 8,000 feet (2,400 m) high in the mountains.

What sights would you like to see where you live?

LET'S GO!

Make a rain forest

You'll need:

a clean 2-liter soda bottle

scissors

tape

small stones or pebbles

potting soil

plants that like moisture (moss, spider plants, or miniature ferns work well)

water

decorative rocks, animal figures, bits of bark (optional)

1

Ask an adult to cut off the top part of the bottle. Save the top. Use tape to cover the sharp edge.

2

Sprinkle a thin layer of pebbles over the bottom of the bottle.

3

Fill the bottle a little more than halfway with soil. Make a small hole in the soil for the plants.

4

Place the plants in the hole. Fill around them with soil.

SOUTH AMERICA

5

To make your rain forest look more realistic, add some pebbles, rocks, animal figures, or bits of bark.

6

Water the plants by dampening the soil. Don't overwater.

7

Tape the top back onto the bottle, leaving the cap off. Place the rain forest in a bottle in a sunny spot.

CHAPTER 3
EUROPE

THE CITY OF LONDON, ENGLAND

Where old meets new

THE COUNTRIES
Countries of all sizes

Europe is the second smallest continent. But it has lots of countries. Many of the major cities are on the coasts or along Europe's long rivers.

Russia's lands stretch from Europe into Asia. Since Russia's major cities are in Europe, it's counted as a European country.

FACTS

COUNTRIES
46

LARGEST COUNTRY
Russia

SMALLEST COUNTRY
Vatican City

CITY WITH THE MOST PEOPLE
Moscow, Russia. 12 million people live there.

ST. BASIL'S CATHEDRAL, MOSCOW, RUSSIA

THE LAND

Long rivers and curvy coastlines

Europe has a lot of coastline. It wraps around many different types of bodies of water.

There are bays, seas, and gulfs. Long rivers crisscross the continent. People have used these waterways to trade goods for thousands of years.

FACTS

SIZE
3,841,000 square miles
(9,947,000 sq km)

HIGHEST MOUNTAIN
El'brus, Russia

LOWEST PLACE
Caspian Sea

LONGEST RIVER
Volga River, Russia

LARGEST LAKE
Lake Ladoga, Russia

Can you spot Europe's four major rivers? They're the Rhine, the Danube, the Rhône, and the Volga.

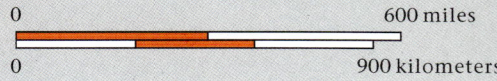

BLACK FOREST IN GERMANY

A BEACH ON THE GREEK ISLAND OF CRETE

EUROPE

THE WEATHER
Mostly mild with plenty of rain

Warm winds blow over Europe from the Atlantic Ocean. This gives much of the continent mild weather. The land is good for farming and raising animals.

Near the Mediterranean Sea, it's warm and sunny all year-round. In the far north, it can get very cold during winter.

SHEEP IN ARCOS DE LA FRONTERA, SPAIN

THE PEOPLE
Many countries, many languages

There are many different groups of people living in Europe. More than 50 languages are spoken here. That's more than one per country!

AN ICELANDIC GIRL WITH HER LAMB

Europe has a long history. The land was once divided among many kingdoms and empires.

Children in Switzerland often study three languages in school—German, English, and French or Italian.

EUROPE

Imagine going to school in a gondola! If you could ride to school in any way, how would you do it?

GONDOLAS IN VENICE, ITALY

51

RED SQUIRREL

This eagle owl is one of the world's largest owl species.

Owls are expert hunters. Some can even take on larger prey such as foxes, opossums, and hares.

EUROPE

THE ANIMALS

Feathery owls and feisty squirrels

Many animals make their homes in the forests of Europe. Rabbits, squirrels, and owls are common.

ALPINE MARMOT

Reindeer and caribou are the same animal! They are known as reindeer in Europe and caribou in North America.

Otters snack on fish in the streams and lakes. In the north, you can find reindeer and arctic fox. Alpine marmots dig winter burrows in the slopes of the Alps.

REINDEER

THE SIGHTS
Stepping into history

People who lived long ago built many of the famous places throughout Europe. Stonehenge is a circle of arranged rocks in England. People built it more than 4,000 years ago. It may have helped them study the stars.

THE COLOSSEUM IN ROME, ITALY

Ancient Romans packed Rome's Colosseum to watch events such as gladiator fights.

EUROPE

STONEHENGE IN ENGLAND

Disneyland's Sleeping Beauty Castle is modeled after Neuschwanstein Castle in Germany.

Castles were once the homes of kings and other wealthy people. One small town in Italy had 72 castles at one time!

EXPLORER SPOTLIGHT

Carsten Peter visits explosive volcanoes.

Carsten Peter wears a heatproof suit. He follows scientists into the mouth of Mount Etna. It's one of the world's most active volcanoes. Mount Etna is on the island of Sicily in Italy.

EUROPE

Carsten's job is to take pictures of an eruption. He joins scientists as they study erupting volcanoes. The scientists want to gather samples of the melted rock, or lava. It's dangerous work. The temperature can climb to 2000°F (1093°C). Dangerous gases fill the air.

Why take the risks? Because no one knows when volcanoes will pop. Explosions can be deadly for the people living near a volcano's slopes. Information from these studies can help save lives.

LET'S GO!

Be an artist like Michelangelo

Michelangelo was a famous European artist. He painted the ceiling of the Sistine Chapel in Vatican City 500 years ago. The paintings are some of the most famous European artworks. Create your own masterpiece the way Michelangelo did! Ask for an adult's help and permission first.

1 Ask an adult to help you set up your art project.

2 Tape the paper to the bottom of the kitchen table. Make sure the writing tools you're going to use do not bleed through the paper onto the table.

You'll need:
- large sheet(s) of paper
- tape
- crayons, colored pencils, or washable markers
- kitchen table or card table

CHAPTER 4
ASIA

THE TAJ MAHAL IN AGRA, INDIA

The world's largest continent

THE COUNTRIES
Lots of land, lots of people

Everything seems bigger in Asia. More people live here than anywhere else on Earth. You'll find the most crowded cities here. Shanghai in China is home to 24 million people.

The city of Tokyo in Japan has the world's busiest metro train system.

FACTS

COUNTRIES
46

LARGEST COUNTRY
China

SMALLEST COUNTRY
Maldives

CITY WITH THE MOST PEOPLE
Tokyo, Japan. 38 million people live there.

A FISHER IN SHANGHAI, CHINA

Most of Turkey is located in Asia, but the northwest part of the country lies in Europe.

THE LAND
Rooftop of the world

You'll find ten of the world's tallest mountain peaks in Asia. They're all in one large mountain chain called the Himalaya.

Rain forests and green valleys appear south of these mountains. The land is frozen for most of the year in the north. Thirsty deserts make up most of central Asia.

MOUNT EVEREST, CHINA-NEPAL BORDER

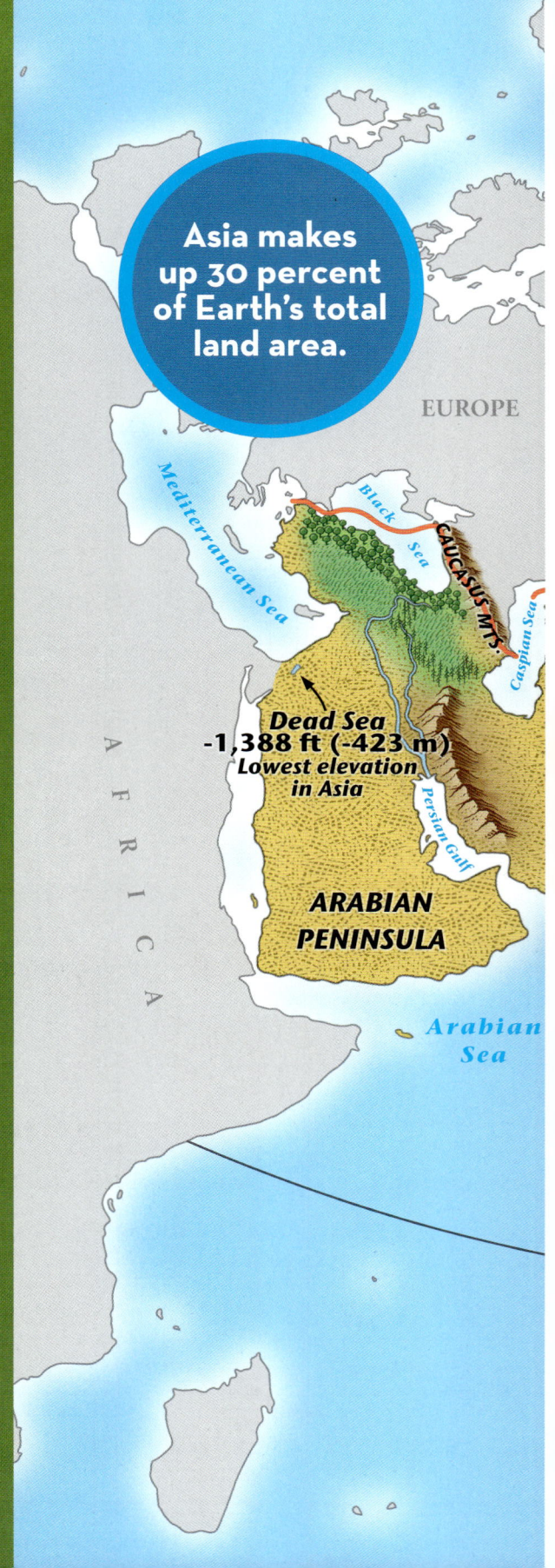

Asia makes up 30 percent of Earth's total land area.

Dead Sea -1,388 ft (-423 m) Lowest elevation in Asia

RIDING THROUGH THE RAIN IN VIETNAM

THE GOBI IN MONGOLIA DURING WINTER

A TEA PLANTATION IN MALAYSIA

ASIA

THE WEATHER

Very cold or hot; very rainy or very dry

Northern Asia has long, icy winters and short, cool summers. It rarely rains in the deserts in Asia's central and western parts.

In the south, heavy rains soak the land in the summer. The rains allow farmers to grow water-loving crops like rice.

Most of the world's rice is grown in Asia.

A RICE PADDY

THE PEOPLE
Land of many traditions

KIDS AT SCHOOL IN THAILAND

Many different groups of people live in Asia. They each have their own language and culture. Some traditions are very old.

The world's first cities were built here thousands of years ago.

WAITING FOR A BUS IN INDIA

ASIA

Millions of people visit Mecca, Saudi Arabia, every year for a religious journey. The tradition is part of the Muslim faith and is called a hajj. It's the world's largest gathering.

A PILGRIMAGE AT MECCA IN SAUDI ARABIA

What are your family's favorite traditions?

A Bengal tiger's roar can be heard up to two miles (3 km) away.

Fuzzy pandas live only in the bamboo forests of China.

ASIA

THE ANIMALS

Lizards, tigers, and bears!

Tigers prowl the forests of India and some other parts of Asia. The world's largest lizard lives in Asia. It's called the Komodo dragon.

KOMODO DRAGON

YAK

Woolly yaks live high up in the Himalaya.

THE SIGHTS

Ancient temples, super skyscrapers, and a great wall

Temples and the ruins of old cities can be found throughout Asia. Angkor Wat in Cambodia is a huge temple that was built over 900 years ago.

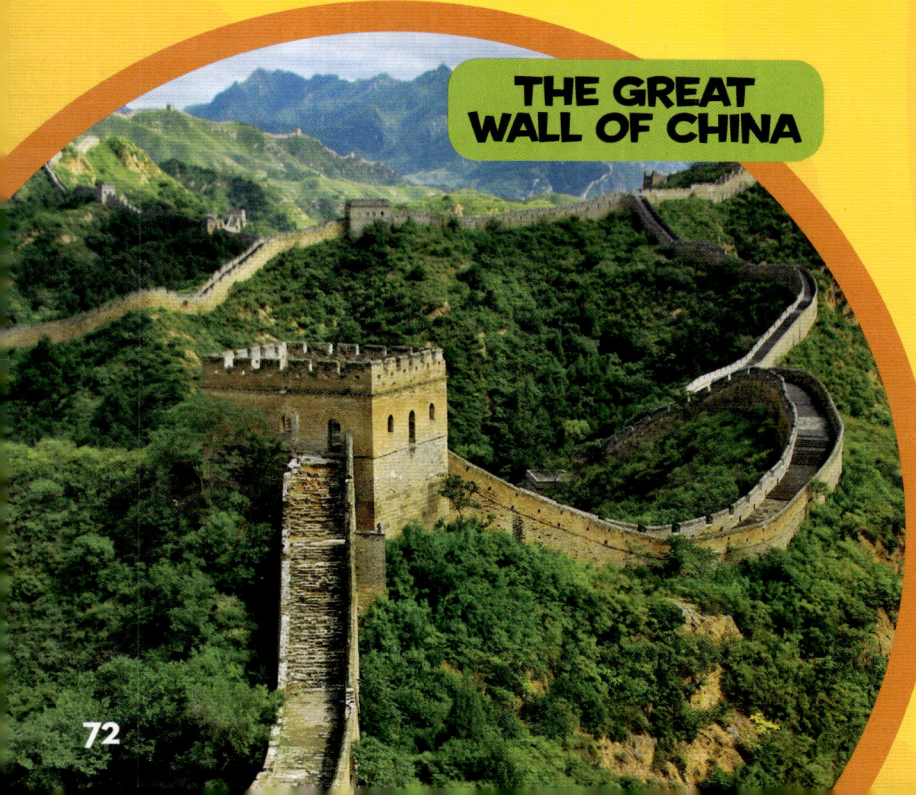

THE GREAT WALL OF CHINA

China's Great Wall is the largest structure built by humans. It was built in sections over hundreds of years. The wall is 13,000 miles (20,921 km) long!

ASIA

Angkor Wat in Cambodia was originally a Hindu temple. Its name means "city of temples."

Burj Khalifa in the United Arab Emirates is a new marvel. It's the world's tallest skyscraper. It's as tall as nine Statues of Liberty stacked on top of each other.

THE BURJ KHALIFA BUILDING

LET'S GO!
Design a mosaic

Some sites in Asia are famous for their mosaics. These beautiful, patterned tiles decorate places like the Blue Mosque in Turkey and the Taj Mahal in India. You can make your own mosaic!

You'll need:
- pencil
- ruler
- scissors
- colored construction paper cut into a variety of shapes, such as triangles, diamonds, pentagons, squares (Draw the shapes on the paper first. Make sure that each shape is the same size and that you have enough of each to make a repeating pattern.)
- 3 or more pieces of cardboard
- glue

ASIA

1. Arrange the pattern blocks or shapes on one cardboard square. Once you're happy with the design, glue the shapes to the square. This is one "tile."

2. You can make as many tiles as you like.

3. Put the tiles together. Count how many different shapes you used in your mosaic. Which shape did you use the most?

CHAPTER 5
AFRICA

A HERD OF ELEPHANTS IN KENYA

Life on the move

THE COUNTRIES
The most of any continent

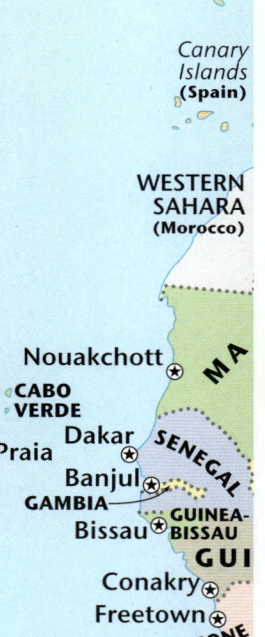

Of all the continents, Africa is divided into the most countries.

The newest country is South Sudan. It was created in 2011.

Africa has 18,500 miles (30,000 km) of coastline.

A boy carries a tray of fresh bread through busy streets in Cairo, Egypt.

Some cities are very crowded. But most Africans live in smaller villages and farms.

FACTS

COUNTRIES
54

LARGEST COUNTRY
Algeria

SMALLEST COUNTRY
Seychelles

CITY WITH THE MOST PEOPLE
Cairo, Egypt. 18 million people live there.

THE LAND

Dry deserts in the north and south, lush forests in the middle

Most of Africa is on a high, flat plateau. There aren't many mountains here. Most craggy peaks are in the east.

You'll find deserts at the northern and southern parts of Africa. A band of forests and grasslands called savannas make up the middle.

ZEBRAS IN TANZANIA

FACTS

SIZE
11,608,000 square miles
(30,065,000 sq km)

HIGHEST MOUNTAIN
Kilimanjaro, Tanzania

LOWEST PLACE
Lake Assal, Djibouti

LONGEST RIVER
Nile River

LARGEST LAKE
Lake Victoria

A RAIN FOREST IN UGANDA

KILIMANJARO, TANZANIA

AFRICA

THE WEATHER
Dry, hot, and rainy

Most places in Africa are very hot. The continent doesn't have any cold-weather environments. It's rainy in the middle of Africa. You'll find rain forests there. North Africa contains the world's largest hot desert—the Sahara.

CAMEL CARAVAN IN THE SAHARA

Strong winds in the Sahara can cause sand storms.

How would you stay cool in the desert?

THE PEOPLE
Our ancient origins

NAIROBI, KENYA

People have lived in Africa longer than any other place. Scientists think that humans came from here.

STUDENTS IN SWAZILAND

Today, many groups of people live in Africa. Some focus on farming and herding. Others live in booming cities where there are lots of businesses.

MASAI CHILDREN IN FRONT OF A MUD HUT, MASAI MARA, KENYA

Masai houses are usually circular or star-shaped.

AFRICA

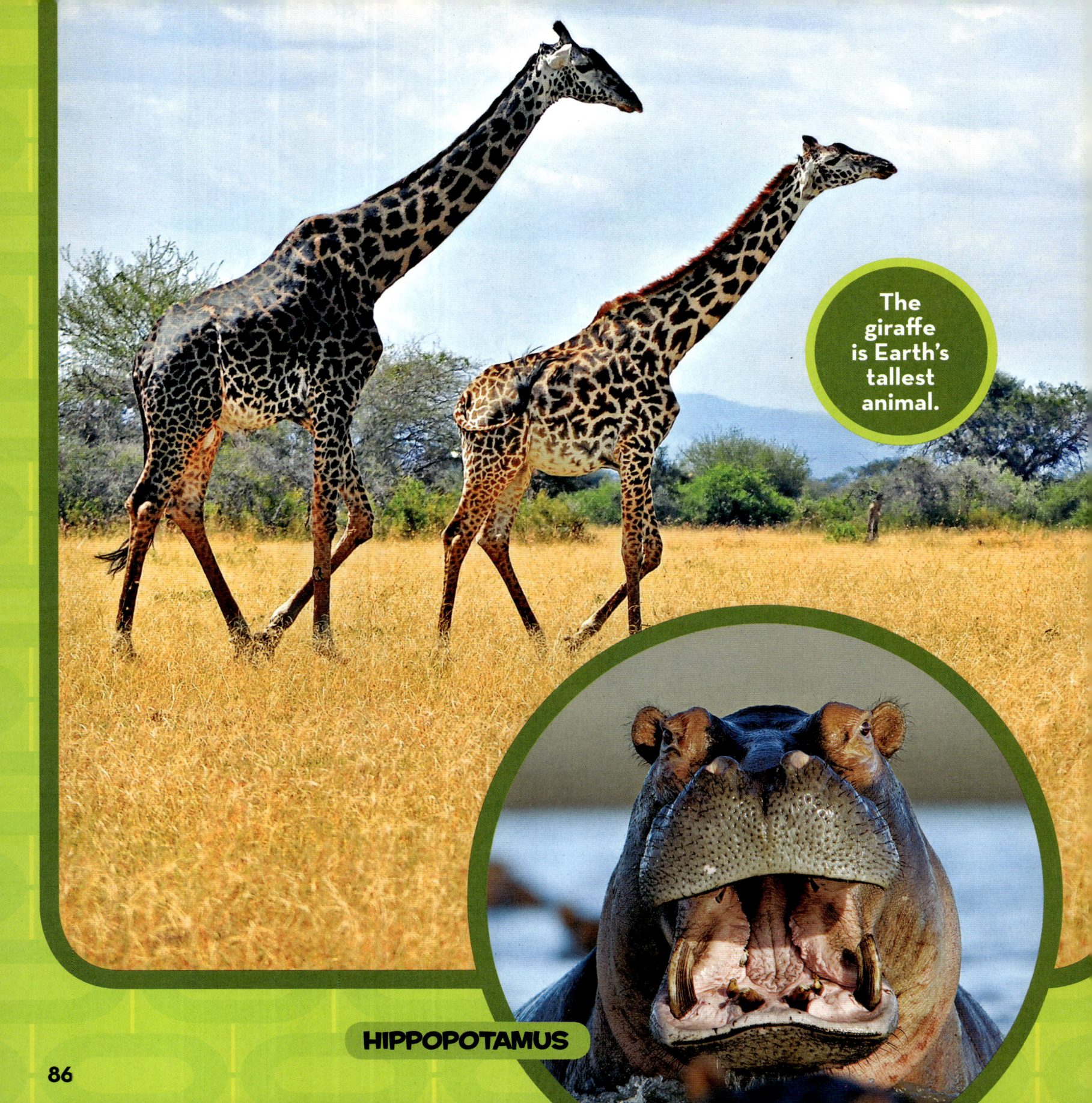

The giraffe is Earth's tallest animal.

HIPPOPOTAMUS

AFRICA

THE ANIMALS
Time for a safari!

Africa is famous for its animal life. You'll find herds of elephants, prides of lions, and towers of giraffes.

A MOTHER LION AND HER CUBS

In the forests of central Africa, gorillas munch peacefully on leaves.

Hungry hippos wade through the rivers and lakes.

GORILLA

THE SIGHTS
Pyramids, wildlife, and waterfalls

Visitors are awed by Egypt's Great Sphinx and pyramids. The ancient Egyptians built them 4,500 years ago.

Every zebra has its own unique stripe pattern.

GREAT PYRAMID AT GIZA, EGYPT

Animal lovers go to the grasslands to see Africa's great animal herds.

AFRICA

VICTORIA FALLS, ZAMBEZI RIVER, ZIMBABWE

Victoria Falls is one of Africa's natural wonders. Its African name means "smoke that thunders." The falls create mist that can be spotted from more than 12 miles (19 km) away.

EXPLORER SPOTLIGHT

Jane Goodall uncovers the world of chimpanzees.

In 1960, Jane Goodall traveled to Africa, packing a pair of binoculars and a notebook. She wanted to learn everything she could about chimpanzees. These apes are humans' closest animal relatives.

AFRICA

Jane lived near chimps in the forests and went to watch them every day. She observed their behavior and took notes. She made many new discoveries. Her work turned into one of the longest studies of chimpanzee behavior.

The descendants of the chimps Jane studied in the 1960s still live in Gombe National Park.

LET'S GO!
Watch animals like a scientist

Jane Goodall made important discoveries about animals by simply watching them. Make a field guide of animal life in your neighborhood.

1 Take your supplies into your backyard or on a walk through your neighborhood. (Get an adult's permission first.)

2 Note the animals you see. What are they doing? What are they eating? Note if animals interact with each other. You can use your colored pencils to draw pictures of them, too.

You'll need:
- notebook
- pen or pencil
- colored pencils (optional)
- binoculars (optional)

AFRICA

3 Try to do your observations at the same time each day, or once a week. Write down any changes that take place.

4 After a few weeks or months, go back and look at your notes. Do you notice any changes happening over time?

5 Continue your observations for as long as you like!

93

CHAPTER 6
AUSTRALIA

A RING-TAILED DRAGON LIZARD IN SHARK BAY, AUSTRALIA

The land down under

THE COUNTRIES

Australia is a country and a continent in one.

Australia is the smallest of the seven continents. It makes up just 5 percent of Earth's land.

BLUE-WINGED KOOKABURRA

It is the only continent that is also a country. It is made up of six states. Australia is called "the land down under" because the whole country is south of, or "under," the Equator.

WESTERN AUSTRALIA

INDIAN OCEAN

FACTS

COUNTRIES
1

STATE WITH THE MOST PEOPLE
New South Wales

STATE WITH THE FEWEST PEOPLE
Tasmania

CITY WITH THE MOST PEOPLE
Sydney. 4.5 million people live there.

THE LAND

A dry and flat outback and thousands of islands

FACTS

SIZE
2,989,000 square miles
(7,741,000 sq km)

HIGHEST MOUNTAIN
Mount Kosciuszko

LOWEST PLACE
Lake Eyre

LONGEST RIVER
Darling River

LARGEST LAKE
Lake Eyre, but it's rarely full of water and is dry for part of the year.

A mountain range runs down Australia's east coast. It blocks rain from the Pacific Ocean. The rest of the continent is dry and flat. The interior is nicknamed the outback.

Eucalyptus and acacia trees are the most common plants found in Australia. Tasmania has large areas of rain forests and mountains.

ULURU

LIMESTONE ROCK TOWERS IN THE AUSTRALIAN DESERT

MILLAA MILLAA FALLS IN QUEENSLAND, AUSTRALIA

AUSTRALIA

THE WEATHER

Sunscreen is a must!

Most of Australia is warm and sunny all the time. Ocean winds bring rain to the coasts. This causes thick forests to grow in some areas.

Hurricanes are a summer weather threat in the region. In this part of the world, hurricanes have a different name. They are called cyclones.

A STORM OVER SYDNEY HARBOR

THE PEOPLE
Ocean crossers on the move

Aboriginals first came to Australia from Asia about 40,000 years ago. They have one of the world's oldest cultures. Storytelling, painting, and dance are all important parts of their lives.

Today, most Australians are related to settlers from Europe who first arrived about 200 years ago. English is the main language.

ABORIGINAL GIRLS WITH FACE PAINT

AUSTRALIA

A SURFING COMPETITION IN SYDNEY, AUSTRALIA

Australian cattle ranches are called stations. There are many across the country.

THE ANIMALS
Kangaroo crossing!

GREEN SEA TURTLE

KOALA

Many unusual animals live in Australia. Koalas, kangaroos, and wallabies raise their babies in pouches in their bellies. The duck-billed platypus is a mammal like us. But its babies hatch out of eggs!

PLATYPUS

Green sea turtles are found off the coast and sometimes come up on land to get some sun.

AUSTRALIA

WALLABIES

CROWN-OF-THORNS SEA STAR

In the coral reefs of the Great Barrier Reef, crown-of-thorns sea stars have become a problem. They hurt the underwater environment by eating corals.

THE SIGHTS
Fun in the water and on land

SURFER AT SNAPPER ROCKS, GOLD COAST

The Great Barrier Reef is Earth's largest living structure. It's off Australia's northeastern coast. Australia's beautiful beaches are popular surfing spots. There's even a city named Surfers Paradise!

SYDNEY OPERA HOUSE

Would you rather learn how to surf or scuba dive?

AUSTRALIA

THE GREAT BARRIER REEF

The Sydney Opera House is one of Australia's most famous places to visit. It hosts plays, dances, and concerts.

LET'S GO!

Leap like a kangaroo

Red kangaroos can cover 25 feet (7.6 m) in a single leap. How does your longest leap compare to a jumping roo's?

You'll need:
- masking tape
- tape measure
- flat ground
- marker

RED KANGAROO

1 Make a line on the ground with masking tape. This is the starting point of your jump.

2 Get a running start and jump from the line you just made. Remember to practice your jumping safely.

AUSTRALIA

3 Mark your landing spot with a piece of tape. Use the tape measure to measure the distance between the starting line and your landing spot.

4 Make several jumps and mark each jump with a piece of tape.

5 Label each try, "Jump 1," "Jump 2," "Jump 3," and so on.

6 Which jump was the longest? How does it measure up to a red kangaroo's?

CHAPTER 7
ANTARCTICA

ANTARCTICA

GENTOO PENGUINS ON AN ICEBERG IN THE ANTARCTIC PENINSULA

Can you feel the chill?

THE LAND
A frozen landscape

Antarctica is Earth's coldest, driest, and windiest place. This landmass covers the South Pole.

There are no countries. But scientists from all over the world have set up research stations here to study the land, weather, and animals.

ATLANTIC OCEAN

PACIFIC OCEAN

FACTS
SIZE
5,100,000 square miles
(13,209,000 sq km)

HIGHEST MOUNTAIN
Vinson Massif

LOWEST PLACE
Byrd Glacier

Antarctica is the world's largest cold desert.

What's your favorite season?

OLYMPUS RANGE IN VICTORIA LAND, ANTARCTICA

The Olympus mountain range surrounds Antarctica's Dry Valleys.

These valleys get their name from the high winds that constantly blast away snow, leaving the land bare.

ANTARCTICA

THE WEATHER
Pack your coat!

It's no surprise—it is cold in Antarctica year-round. Temperatures rarely rise above freezing. The continent gets very little rain or snow. That makes Antarctica a big cold desert.

The thick layer of ice covering the continent actually took millions of years to build up.

A BLIZZARD NEAR THE SOUTH POLE

BLUE-EYED CORMORANT

Sea birds such as penguins (above) and cormorants (left) feast on the plentiful fish that live in the waters around Antarctica.

EMPEROR PENGUINS

ANTARCTICA

THE ANIMALS

It's a penguin parade.

It might seem like nothing could survive in Antarctica. But that's not the case. Some animals are built for life here. Emperor penguins live on Antarctica year-round.

LEOPARD SEAL

HUMPBACK WHALE

Leopard seals hunt among the floating ice.

Blue and humpback whales swim through Antarctic waters in the summer.

EXPLORER SPOTLIGHT

Roald Amundsen was the first explorer to reach the South Pole.

He planted Norway's flag at the South Pole on December 14, 1911. He and his team risked their lives to explore the frozen continent.

ANTARCTICA

They had to drag supplies across 900 miles (1,500 km) of ice and back again. They wore heavy furs. For 99 days, they lived off food such as dried meat, raisins, and cocoa (what chocolate is made of).

Amundsen's success helped people learn more about polar exploration and the conditions in Antarctica.

LET'S GO!
Take care of a penguin "egg"

Mommy and daddy emperor penguins take turns caring for their egg. The penguin parent holds the egg on its feet to keep it warm. Try taking care of your own egg.

You'll need:
one orange

1 Place the orange on your feet. Gently support it by squeezing it with your feet. This is your penguin egg.

2 Now try to walk around like a penguin. Remember to waddle with your feet together, supporting your egg.

PARENT TIPS

YOU CAN REINFORCE AN UNDERSTANDING OF PLACE, DIRECTION, AND MAP READING BEYOND THE PAGES OF THIS BOOK. The time you spend extending these concepts can pay off greatly. Geography can be an abstract concept for children. Often, our kids are magically transported from here to there—usually via the Parent Taxi Service! Involve your child in the planning of routes. Explain directionality using natural markers such as the rising and setting sun and the North Star. City kids can help determine which subway or bus lines to take using your transit system's map.

Here are some other activities you can do after reading National Geographic's *Little Kids First Big Book of the World*.

THREADS OF THE WORLD
(Search Strategy)
Many of the goods that we buy are actually produced and shipped from faraway places. Your child can build a solid understanding of this by rummaging through her closet. With your child, look at the tags on her clothes and note the country where each piece was made. Make a list and mark the locations on the world map in this book. Discuss any trends you notice with your child. Did more clothes come from any particular continent?

GEO JAMS
(Music)
Explore the origins of the music you listen to in your home. What kinds of instruments are used to make your child's favorite tunes? Where do they come from? Drums and shakers are great examples of instruments that are made differently depending on a people's culture and location. For example, Inuit musicians make drums out of wood and caribou skin. During dances, Cherokee women wear leg rattles made of tortoise shells with pebbles inside. Ask your child to draw a picture of an instrument he would create if designing one from scratch. See if you can make the instrument using regular household objects.

BLOCK PARTY
(Math)
Help your child use blocks to make a 3-D map of your neighborhood. Label the block that represents your house, the one that represents your child's school, the neighborhood playground, and so on. Younger children can trace blocks onto paper to make a 2-D map. Then, take the map with you on your next outing. Use it to navigate to your destination. Make a wrong turn? That's a great opportunity to teach your child about the importance of revising your work after you've tested it.

MAPS EVERYWHERE
(Arts and Crafts)
Displaying maps in your home is a great way to incorporate them into your routines. Maps can appear in unexpected places. (Check out shower curtain maps, map placemats, map posters, and map bulletin boards.) Hang a country or world map and insert push pins into all the places your family has visited. Or, have your child interview family members to find out where your family and their ancestors are originally from. Mark these locations on a map and include family pictures, if available. You can even create your own map puzzle. Give your child a map that you don't use and allow her to cut it into jigsaw-shaped pieces.

MAKE A MODEL
(Geography/Landforms)
Use modeling clay to form geographic features, such as islands, mountains, and valleys. If available, make models in a disposable baking dish with plasticine, a type of clay that doesn't absorb water. Pour water into the dish to model the water and land features. For younger kids, make expanding oceans. Draw the seven continents on a coffee filter. Roughly fill in the oceans in blue. Spray water on the filter and watch the blue "water" spread.

GAMES OF THE GLOBE
(Exercise)
Many popular sports originated in other places. With your child, research the roots of his favorite sport. Have the rules and equipment changed since the sport became popular here? If they have, try to organize a pick-up game of the sport that incorporates some of the original rules. For example, if your children's favorite sport is baseball, take a look at how cricket, the sport that inspired baseball, was played. How could you tweak your game to include some of the rules of cricket?

IMAGINARY ISLAND
(Creative Thinking)
Teach your child about map symbols and legends by having her create a map of an imaginary secret island. The island can be the location of anything: a pirate hideout, an alien spaceship landing site, a tropical resort for unicorns—you name it! The map must include symbols and a legend, or key, that explains what each symbol means.

VISIT ONLINE
(Technology)
For more geography education resources and map exploration tools, visit:

education.nationalgeographic.com/education

kids.nationalgeographic.com

nationalgeographic.com/kids-world-atlas/maps.html

GLOSSARY

ATLAS
a book of maps

CARAVAN
a group of people, usually traders, traveling across a desert in Africa or Asia

CLIMATE
the average weather conditions of a place

CONTINENT
one of the world's main expanses of land

DESERT
a dry area of land that receives fewer than ten inches (25 cm) of rain or snow a year

EQUATOR
an imaginary line around the Earth that divides the planet into northern and southern hemispheres, or halves

ERUPTION
the release of lava and/or gas from a vent in a volcano

EXPLORATION
the act of traveling through an unfamiliar area to learn about it

GLACIER
a slowly moving mass of ice usually found high up in mountains or near the poles

GLADIATORS
men trained to fight with weapons against other men or animals for sport

GONDOLA
a flat-bottomed boat that is commonly used as transportation through canals in Venice, Italy

GOODS
items such as food or clothing that are commonly sold in a marketplace

LANDMASS
a large chunk of land, such as a continent or a large island

MAMMAL
a warm-blooded animal whose young feed on milk produced by the mother

MOSAIC
a picture or pattern usually made by arranging pieces of glass or tile

MOSQUE
a place of worship for people of the Muslim religion

MYTHOLOGY
a collection of stories that belong to one culture or religion

OBSERVE
to notice something and believe it's important or figure out that it's not important

PILGRIMAGE
a religious journey usually made to a sacred place

PLATEAU
an area of high ground that is flat

PREY
animals that are hunted and killed by another animal for food

PYRAMID
a large structure with a square or triangular base and sloping sides that meet in a point at the top

RAIN FOREST
a dense forest that receives more than 60 inches (152 cm) of rain a year

SETTLER
a person who moves into an undeveloped area to live there

SPECIES
a group of similar organisms that can produce young

TERRITORY
an area of land under the control of another country's government

VOLCANO
An opening in Earth's crust (usually at the top of a mountain or hill) where lava, ash, and gases from deep inside Earth escape

INDEX

Boldface indicates illustrations.

A
Aboriginals 102, **102**
Africa
  animals **76-77**, 80, 83, **86-87**, 87, 88, **88**, **90-91**
  deserts 80, 83, **83**
  land and weather 80, 83
  maps 78-79, 80-81
  people 78, **78**, 84, **84-85**
  rain forests 82, 83
  savannas 80
Alberta, Canada: bison **10-11**
Alpine marmots 53, **53**
Amazon rain forest, South America 30, 33, **33**
Amazon River, South America 30, **30**
Amundsen, Roald 118-119, **118-119**
Andes (mountains), South America 30, 36
Angkor Wat, Cambodia 72, **72-73**
Antarctica
  animals **110-111**, **116-117**, 117, 120, **120-121**
  land and weather 112, 115
  map 112-113
  polar exploration 118-119, **118-119**
  research stations 112, **112**
Arches National Park, Utah 14
Arcos de la Frontera, Spain 49
Armadillos **36**, 37
Asia
  animals **70-71**, 71
  land and weather 64, 67
  maps 62-63, 64-65
  people **66**, 68, **68-69**
  rice growing 67, **67**
  temples **2-3**, 72, **72-73**
  traditions 68, 69
Atacama Desert, Chile 30, **30**
Australia
  animals **94-95**, 96, 104-105, **104-105**, 108, **108**
  coral reefs 105, 106, **106-107**
  land and weather 98, 101
  maps 96-97, 98-99
  outback 98
  people 102, **102-103**
Ayers Rock (Uluru), Australia 98, **98**

B
Basketball 18, **18**
Bayon Temple, Cambodia **2-3**
Bison **10-11**
Black Forest, Germany **48**
Blue Mosque, Turkey 74, **74-75**
Blue-winged kookaburra **96**
Brazil 29
  jaguar **26-27**
  rain forest 33
  see also Rio de Janeiro
Burj Khalifa, Dubai, United Arab Emirates 73, **73**

C
Cairo, Egypt 78, **78**
Camels 36, **83**
Canada 13
  elk **12**
  see also Alberta; Nunavut
Caribou 53, **53**
Carnival 38, **38**
Castles 55, **55**
Chichén Itzá, Mexico **22**
Chimpanzees 90-91, **90-91**
China 62
  pandas 70, **70**
  see also Great Wall of China; Shanghai
Colosseum, Rome, Italy 54, **54**
Cormorants 116, **116**
Crete (island), Greece 48
Crown-of-thorns sea stars 105, **105**

D
Deserts
  Africa 80, 83, **83**
  Antarctica 112, 115
  Asia 64, **66**
  Australia **100**
  North America 14
  South America 27, 30, **30**
Dry Valleys, Antarctica 114
Duck-billed platypus 104, **104**

E
Ecuador: white-water rafters **34-35**
Egypt
  pyramids 88, **88**
  see also Cairo
Elephants **2-3**, **76-77**, 87
Elk **12**
Emperor penguins **116-117**, 117, 120, **120-121**
England. see London; Stonehenge
Etna, Mount, Sicily, Italy 56, **56-57**
Europe
  animals 49, 50, **52-53**, 53
  history 46, 50, 54-55
  land and weather 46, 49
  major rivers 46
  maps 44-45, 46-47
  people 50, **50-51**, 54
Everest, Mount, China-Nepal **64**, 65

F
Foxes 52, 53

G
Gentoo penguins **110-111**
Giraffes **86**, 87
Glaciers National Park, Argentina 32, **32**
Gobi desert, Asia **66**
Goodall, Jane 90-91, **90-91**, 92
Gorillas 87, **87**
Grand Canyon, Ariz. 22, **22**
Great Barrier Reef, Australia 105, 106, **106-107**
Great Wall of China, China 72, **72**
Green sea turtles 104, **104**
Greenland 12, **14**
Guanacos 36, **36**

H
Himalaya, Asia 64
Hippopotamuses **86**, 87
Humpback whales 117, **117**

I
Iceland: girl with lamb **50**
Inca 38, 39
India **68**, 71; see also Taj Mahal
Italy 54; see also Colosseum; Etna, Mount; Venice

J
Jaguar **26-27**

K
Kangaroos 104, 108, **108**
Kenya
  elephants **76-77**
  see also Masai Mara; Nairobi
Kilimanjaro, Mount, Tanzania 80, **82-83**
Koalas 104, **104**
Komodo dragons 71, **71**

L
Leopard seals 117, **117**

Lions 87, **87**
London, England **42-43**
Los Flamencos National Reserve, Chile 30

M
Macaws **20-21**, 36, **36**, 37
Machu Picchu, Peru 38, **38-39**
Malaysia: tea plantation **66**
Manatees 20, **20**, 21
Masai Mara, Kenya: Masai children **84-85**
Maya 22
Mecca, Saudi Arabia **68-69**, 69
Mexico 12
  beach **16-17**
  pyramids 22, **22**
Michelangelo 58
Millaa Millaa Falls, Queensland, Australia **100-101**
Mongolia: desert **66**
Mont Saint-Michel, France **1**
Mosaics 74-75, **74-75**
Musk oxen 21, **21**

N
Nairobi, Kenya **84**
Neuschwanstein Castle, Germany **55**
North America
  animals **10-11**, 12, **20-21**, 21
  cultures 18
  land and weather 14, 17
  languages 24
  maps 13, 15
  natural wonders 22
  people 18, **18-19**
North Pole 14
Nunavut, Canada: tobogganing **18-19**

O
Olympus Range, Antarctica 114, **114-115**
Owls 52, **52**, 53

P
Pandas 70, **70**
Penguins **110-111**, **116-117**, 117, 120, **120-121**
Peru: stone ruins 38, **38-39**
Peruvian girl **34**
Peter, Carsten 56-57, **56-57**
Pink river dolphins 37, **37**
Poison dart frogs 37, **37**
Polar bears **20-21**, 21

126

Pyramids 22, **22**, 88, **88**, 125

R
Rain forests
  Africa **82**, 83
  Asia 64
  Central America 21
  South America 27, 33, **33**, 37
  Tasmania 98
Reindeer 53, **53**
Ring-tailed dragon lizard **94-95**
Rio de Janeiro, Brazil **28**, 38
Russia 44; *see also* St. Basil's Cathedral

S
Saguaro cactus **14**
Sahara, Africa 83, **83**
Shanghai, China 62, **62**
Shark Bay, Australia **94-95**
Sheep **49**, 50
Sistine Chapel, Vatican City 58
Soccer **34-35**, 35
South America
  animals **26-27, 36-37**, 37
  desert 27, 30, **30**
  land and weather 30, 33
  maps 29, 31
  people 34, **34-35**, 38, **38**
  rain forest 27, 33, **33**, 37
South Pole 112, 115, 118, **118**
Squirrel monkey **21**
Squirrels **52**, 53
St. Basil's Cathedral, Moscow, Russia **44**
Statue of Liberty, New York, N.Y. **22-23**, 23, 73
Stonehenge, England 54, **54-55**
Swaziland: students **84**
Switzerland: students **50**
Sydney, Australia: surfing **102-103**
Sydney Harbor, Sydney, Australia: storm **101**
Sydney Opera House, Sydney, Australia **106**, 107

T
Taj Mahal, Agra, India **60-61**, 74
Tanzania
  mountain **82-83**
  zebras **80**
Tasmania 98
Thailand: students **68**
Tigers **70-71**, 71
Tokyo, Japan 62, **63**

Tornadoes 16, **16**
Tulum, Mexico **16-17**
Tumucumaque National Park, Brazil **33**
Turkey 62; *see also* Blue Mosque

U
Uganda: rain forest **82**
Uluru (Ayers Rock), Australia 98, **98**
United States 12, 23
  tornadoes 16, **16**
  see also Arches National Park; Grand Canyon; Statue of Liberty
Ural Mountains, Europe-Asia 47

V
Venice, Italy: gondolas **50-51**
Vespucci, Amerigo 13
Victoria Falls, Zambia-Zimbabwe **88-89**, 89
Vietnam: bike riders **66**
Volcanoes 30, **56-57, 56-57**, 80, 125

W
Wallabies 104, **104-105**
World: maps 8-9

Y
Yaks 71, **71**

Z
Zebras **80**, 88, **88**

PHOTO CREDITS

ABBREVIATIONS: AL: Alamy; GI: Getty Images; IS: iStockphoto; NGC: National Geographic Creative; SS: Shutterstock

Cover (St Basil's), Vladitto/SS; (Earth), leonello calvetti/SS; (tiger), Benjamin Jessop/IS; (fruit), Lori Epstein/NGC; (Sphinx & pyramid) Ian Stewart/SS; (Asian elephant), Lori Epstein/NGC; (cherry blossoms), Lori Epstein/NGC; (red-eyed tree frog), Mark Kostich/IS; (Statue of Liberty), james cheadle/AL; (Earth), leonello calvetti/SS; (hippo), Roy Toft/NGC; 1, Boris Stroujko/SS; 2-3, Jim Richardson/NGC; 4 (UP), BogdanBoev/SS; 4 (LO), Armando Frazao/SS; 5 (UP), Dave Pusey/SS; 5 (LO), frans lemmens/AL; 10-11, Peter Adams/Photographer's Choice/GI; 12, John E Marriott/All Canada Photos/GI; 14 (UP), PavelSvoboda/SS; 14 (LOLE), Colin D. Young/SS; 14 (LORT), Jo Ann Snover/SS; 16 (INSET), Todd Shoemake/SS; 16, BlueOrange Studio/SS; 17, Lane V. Erickson/SS; 18 (LE), blickwinkel/AL; 18 (RT), Aspen Photo/SS; 19 Design Pics Inc./AL; 20, Tom linster/SS; 20 (LOLE), Greg Amptman/SS; 20 (LORT), Jak Wonderly; 21 (LE), Dennis Jacobsen/SS; 21 (RT), Mikhail Blajenov/SS; 22 (LE), Martin M303/SS; 22 (RT), Patryk Kosmider/SS; 23, Mike Tauber/Blend Images RM/GI; 24-25 (kids), Christopher Futcher/iStockphoto; 24-25 (UP), barbaliss/SS; 25 (music notes), argus/Shutterstock; 26-27, Mint Images/Art Wolfe/GI; 28, Catarina Belova/SS; 31 (UP), Steven Vidler/Eurasia Press/Corbis; 31 (LO), Nataliya Hora/SS; 32, elnavegante/SS; 33, Aaron Chervenak/AL; 34 (LE), Bartosz Hadyniak/Vetta/GI; 34 (RT), Ammit Jack/SS; 35, Digital Media Pro/SS; 36 (UP), David Thyberg/SS; 36 (LOLE), WitthayaP/SS; 36 (LORT), Marcos Amend/SS; 37 (LE), guentermaraus/SS; 37 (RT), Dirk Ercken/SS; 38, T photography/SS; 39, Lori Epstein/NGC; 40 (All), Lori Epstein/www.loriepstein.com; 41 (All), Lori Epstein/www.loriepstein.com; 42-43 Pawel Libera/Stone Sub/GI; 44, Tatiana Popova/SS; 48, Tom Plesnik/SS; 48 (INSET), Patrick Poendl/SS; 49, Lori Epstein/NGC; 50 (LE), Arctic Images/SS; 50 (RT), BSIP SA/AL; 51, Matthias Scholz/AL; 52 (INSET), seawhisper/SS; 52, blickwinkel/AL; 53 (LE), Andreas Gradin/SS; 53 (RT), Erick Margarita Images/SS; 54, JeniFoto/SS; 55 (UP), Cedric Weber/SS; 55 (LO), Belushi/SS; 56, Carsten Peter/NGC; 57 (UP), Carsten Peter/NGC; 57 (LO), Carsten Peter/NGC; 58, Lori Epstein/www.loriepstein.com; 59 (All), Lori Epstein/www.loriepstein.com; 60-61, Lori Epstein/NGC; 62 (LE), Oktay Ortakcioglu/Vetta/GI; 62 (RT), Sean Pavone/SS; 64, AntonSokolov/SS; 66 (inset UP), Thomas Bradford/IS; 66, David Edwards/NGC; 66 (INSET lo), Iakov Kalinin/SS; 67, Tom Wang/SS; 68 (UP), Hector Conesa/SS; 68 (LO), Lori Epstein/NGC; 69, Zurijeta/SS; 70, neelsky/SS; 70 (INSET), Hung Chung Chih/SS; 71 (LE), seastudio/IS; 71 (RT), Anna Kucherova/SS; 72, feiyuezhangjie/SS; 73 (LE), Luciano Mortula/IS; 73 (RT), Sophie James/SS; 74 (All), Oleg Golovnev/SS; 74-75, Matej Kastelic/SS; 75 (all INSETs), Lori Epstein/www.loriepstein.com; 76-77, Martin Harvey/Photolibrary RM/GI; 78, Lori Epstein/NGC; 80, fStop Images/Sean Russell/Brand X/GI; 82 (INSET), Boleslaw Kubica/SS; 82, Graeme Shannon/SS; 83, cdrin/SS; 84 (LE), Aleksandar Todorovic/SS; 84 (RT), Pal Teravagimov/SS; 85, boezie/IS; 86 (INSET), Roy Toft/NGC; 86, moizhusein/SS; 87 (LE), PRILL/SS; 87 (RT), Dave Pusey/SS; 88 (LE), Gerry Ellis/Digital Vision; 88 (RT), Iexan/SS; 89, Przemyslaw Skibinski/SS; 90, Hugo Van Lawick/NGC; 91 (UP), Michael Nichols/NGC; 91 (LO), Michael Nichols/NGC; 92, Lori Epstein/www.loriepstein.com; 93 (All), Lori Epstein/www.loriepstein.com; 94-95, Paul Morton/E+/GI; 96, imageBROKER/AL; 98, Simon Bradfield/IS; 100, Wouter Tolenaars/SS; 100 (INSET), ck10_9/IS; 101, CristinaMuraca/SS; 102, Penny Tweedie/GI; 103, frans lemmens/AL; 103 (INSET), LOOK Die Bildagentur der Fotografen GmbH/AL; 104 (UP), Stephen Frink/Digital Vision; 104 (CTR), Martin Valigursky/SS; 104 (LO), John Carnemolla/IS; 105 (UP), Richard l'Anson/Lonely Planet Images/GI; 105 (LO), WaterFrame/AL; 106 (LE), GTS Production/SS; 106 (RT), Selfiy/SS 107, David Doubilet/NGC; 108 (LE), Dirk Freder/IS; 108 (RT), Lori Epstein/www.loriepstein.com; 109 (All), Lori Epstein/www.loriepstein.com; 110-111, Wayne Lynch/All Canada Photos/GI; 112, Gordon Wiltsie/NGC; 114, Maria Stenzel/NGC; 115, Gordon Wiltsie/NGC; 116, Maria Stenzel/NGC; 116 (INSET), Dmytro Pylypenko/SS; 117 (LE), Keenpress/NGC; 117 (RT), Paul Nicklen/NGC; 118, Public Domain; 119 (LE), NOAA; 119 (CTR), Public Domain; 119 (RT), Public Domain; 120 (All), Lori Epstein/www.loriepstein.com; 121, Graham Robertson/Minden Pictures; 124, Pal Teravagimov/SS; 125, Tom linster/SS; 127, majeczka/SS

Published by Collins
An imprint of HarperCollins Publishers
1 Robroyston Gate,
Glasgow
G33 1JN
www.harpercollins.co.uk

HarperCollins Publishers
Macken House
39/40 Mayor Street Upper
Dublin 1
D01 C9W8
Ireland

© 2015 National Geographic Partners LLC. All rights reserved.
NATIONAL GEOGRAPHIC KIDS and Yellow Border Design are trademarks of National Geographic Society, used under license.

First published 2015
This edition 2026

ISBN 9780008825218

10 9 8 7 6 5 4 3 2 1

All rights reserved. No part of this publication may be reproduced, stored in a retrieval system, or transmitted, in any form or by any means, electronic, mechanical, photocopying, recording or otherwise without the prior permission in writing of the publisher and copyright owners.

Without limiting the exclusive rights of any author, contributor or the publisher of this publication, any unauthorised use of this publication to train generative artificial intelligence (AI) technologies is expressly prohibited. HarperCollins also exercise their rights under Article 4(3) of the Digital Single Market Directive 2019/790 and expressly reserve this publication from the text and data mining exception.

The contents of this publication are believed correct at the time of printing. Nevertheless the publisher can accept no responsibility for errors or omissions, changes in the detail given or for any expense or loss thereby caused.

HarperCollins does not warrant that any website mentioned in this title will be provided uninterrupted, that any website will be error free, that defects will be corrected, or that the website or the server that makes it available are free of viruses or bugs. For full terms and conditions please refer to the site terms provided on the website.

A catalogue record for this book is available from the British Library

Printed in India

If you would like to comment on any aspect of this book, please contact us at the above address or online.
natgeokidsbooks.co.uk
collins.reference@harpercollins.co.uk

Staff for This Book
Priyanka Sherman, Amy Briggs, Project Editors
Eva Absher-Schantz, Art Director
Lori Epstein, Senior Photo Editor
Carl Mehler, Director of Maps
Juan José Valdés, The Geographer
Martha Sharma, Geography Consultant
Paige Towler, Editorial Assistant
Maureen J. Flynn, Julie A. Ibinson, Michael Fry, Map Editors
Michael McNey and Martin S. Walz, Map Production
Erica Holsclaw, Special Projects Assistant
Rachel Kenny, Design Production Assistant
Michael Cassady, Rights Clearance Specialist
Grace Hill, Managing Editor
Joan Gossett, Senior Production Editor
Lewis R. Bassford, Production Manager
George Bounelis, Manager, Production Services
Susan Borke, Legal and Business Affairs

Senior Management Team, Kids Publishing and Media
Nancy Laties Feresten, Senior Vice President
Jennifer Emmett, Vice President, Editorial Director, Kids Books
Julie Vosburgh Agnone, Vice President, Editorial Operations
Rachel Buchholz, Editor and Vice President, NG Kids magazine
Michelle Sullivan, Vice President, Kids Digital
Eva Absher-Schantz, Design Director
Jay Sumner, Photo Director
Hannah August, Marketing Director
R. Gary Colbert, Production Director

Digital
Anne McCormack, Director
Laura Goertzel, Sara Zeglin, Producers
Jed Winer, Special Projects Assistant
Emma Rigney, Creative Producer
Brian Ford, Video Producer
Bianca Bowman, Assistant Producer
Natalie Jones, Senior Product Manager